Contents

Introduction

Whatever the technology available, in the end all wars are fought by individuals. The men and women who served in World War II faced hardship and danger but also often enjoyed camaraderie and excitement.

Although all the available figures are estimates, it is likely that up to 85 million people around the world performed military service during World War II. The precise nature of their service varied immensely. Although large numbers fought with the army, many more also served on naval vessels or in aircraft. There were specialized artillery and tank crews. Most armies even had cavalry detachments that still relied on horsepower. There was a long list of support roles, too, from medics, surgeons and nurses to quartermasters, members of the signal corps and drivers. The U.S. Construction Battalions ('Seebees'), for example, were engineers and builders who constructed the airfields and bases that enabled the American fighting forces to advance across the Pacific.

Shared Experience

Although the individual experiences of the men and women who served varied greatly, depending on their roles and what country they came from, there were some elements that were common to nearly everyone who took part. They all had to leave their homes, often travelling to distant countries and continents. They exchanged their families and friends for the colleagues in the units in which they served. They were subject to new forms of discipline and chains of command that they often found irritating. They found that they lost the ability to make their own choices: they became part of a larger system. Not all of them faced danger, and certainly not all of the time, but most did to a greater or lesser extent.

Soldier Life

Some people who joined the war were volunteers eager to 'do their bit' for their country; others were reluctant conscripts, who were ordered into military service. Some had specialized skills; others were expected to do little more than point a rifle and shoot. But all had to be recruited into the services and trained for their duties. They all had to be entertained and to have their morale maintained even in the face of adversity. They all had to be physically cared for, especially if they were wounded or sick. And at the war's end, most had to return to their civilian lives. This book outlines some of these shared experiences of the men and women who took part in the war.

This U.S. poster reflects one of the primary concerns of all fighting forces: to make sure that the men and women on active service were fit and healthy enough to do their jobs.

Recruitment

The number of individuals involved in the war was enormous – 16 million in the United States military services alone. Many were forcibly recruited.

On all sides, the people who fought ended up in the military in one of two ways: they volunteered for one reason or another; or they were conscripted, or forced to serve by law.

A Huge Increase in Numbers

The war required huge numbers of participants to fight in the front line, serve on naval or merchant ships, fly and service aircraft, staff hospitals and medical centres, provide support services for front-line troops, drive trucks and so on. Between the start of the war in 1939 and its end in 1945 national armies doubled and tripled in size. From fewer than 900,000 men in 1939, the British army rose to 3.5 million by 1945 (in all, Britain and its empire had 8.7 million people in uniform); in Germany, the army increased during the course of the war from about 800,000 to something approaching 6 million at the surrender in 1945, by which time its total military services numbered nearly 11 million.

SUPPORT SERVICES
Many individuals did not have front-line roles. The military required a vast infrastructure (organisational systems) for transportation and care of the fighting men. It included, for example, the famous Seabees, or Construction Battalions, of the U.S. Navy in the Pacific.

VOLUNTEERS

People volunteered for military service for many reasons. One was excitement: the chance to see some action. Another was the need for a job after the Great Depression. Other incentives had more to do with values and beliefs. Some volunteers were passionate about defending their country. Others believed that they were fighting for a cause, particularly the defeat of fascism.

⟹ **Young American volunteers wait to join the navy two days after the Japanese attack on Pearl Harbor in December 1941.**

⇐ The most famous U.S. Army recruiting poster featured 'Uncle Sam'; it was originally designed during World War I by the artist James Montgomery Flagg.

⇓ **This poster encouraged recruits to join the Luftwaffe, the German Air Force. Some 3.4 million Germans served in the Luftwaffe between 1939 and 1945.**

MOBILISATION

Mobilisation is the process of getting armies into the field ready to fight in the face of an approaching war. In Germany and Japan, militaristic governments began the process of mobilisation in the 1930s; the Japanese army invaded Manchuria in 1931, while Adolf Hitler encouraged the army to practice manoeuvres. In the Soviet Union, Stalin mobilized troops in the east to discourage Japanese expansion in East Asia. Although the western Allies – Britain and France – had mobilisation plans, war came so rapidly that they did not have time to put them into practice before the German Blitzkrieg swept through Europe.

At the start of the war, most countries had small, professional armies composed of volunteers. Many of the officer corps had experienced active service in World War I (1914–1918). Most armies could also call on supplies of reservists. These were either older veterans who had done military service in the recent past or were volunteers who had had some military training but only served part-time, holding down civilian jobs at the same time.

Militarisation

As the conflict approached, however, governments had begun to take steps to increase the numbers. In Germany, Adolf Hitler's Nazi government started remilitarizing the country in 1935, despite being forbidden to do so by the Versailles Treaty of 1919, which had punished Germany for causing World War I. Hitler ordered the building of new warships and aircraft and also increased the number of men in the

U.S. ARMY AIR FORCES

<== A new pilot's 'wings' shine on his chest in this U.S. recruiting poster. The U.S. Army Air Force came into being in June 1940 and grew rapidly after Germany's Blitzkrieg in Europe proved how effective air power could be.

RESERVED OCCUPATIONS

Some men were exempt from military service because of their jobs. Reserved occupations in Britain, for example, included professionals such as scientists, bank employees, company directors and vets; it also included miners, farmers, railway workers, merchant seamen and people who worked for utility services such as water or electricity. Policemen were also exempt, as were priests and students... but only until they completed their studies.

⇓ Policemen and railway employees, seen here accompanying young evacuees arriving at a rural station in England in 1939, were both on the British list of reserved occupations.

military, or Wehrmacht. In Japan, too, a highly militaristic government was increasing the number of personnel on active duty.

Start of the War

At the start of the war in Europe, German forces had been gathering for months; by contrast, Allied armies were in a poor state of readiness. When Germany invaded Poland in September 1939, the Polish forces were easily overrun. Poland's allies, France and Britain, barely had time to mobilise their forces before Poland was defeated and France itself was under threat.

SPANISH CIVIL WAR

The Spanish Civil War began in 1936 when General Francisco Franco led a coup following the election of a Republican government. Franco's Nationalists fought the Republicans, who were supported by volunteers from other countries. Franco's forces, including German and Italian units, won victory in 1939.

Volunteers

The outbreak of war had an immediate effect on recruitment. The desire to resist enemy invasion encouraged volunteers in those countries in immediate peril, such as Poland and Belgium. In other Allied countries large numbers of people volunteered with a mixture of motives.

Some saw fascism as an evil that had to be resisted. Volunteers from Britain, the United States and other countries had already fought against the Nationalists in the Spanish Civil War (1936–1939). Now volunteers like, for example, U.S. pilots who fought in the Battle of Britain, were motivated by similar beliefs.

Other volunteers were determined to preserve their homeland, either because it had already been invaded – like France – or because it seemed in imminent danger, as in Great Britain. Volunteer numbers

In the Soviet Union, meanwhile, Stalin believed that the Soviet-German Pact of 1939 would allow the Soviet Union to stay out of the war for as long as possible. Against the advice of his generals, he worried that mobilizing troops on the western border would provoke a German attack. When that attack came in June 1941, Soviet forces were caught off guard and were ill prepared to mount a defence.

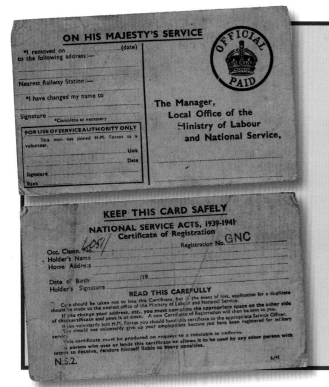

CONSCRIPTION

Conscription – the forced recruitment of citizens into the armed forces – had been used on a large scale in World War I (1914–1918). In World War II it was eventually adopted by all major combatants when it became clear that volunteer armies would not be big enough to fight a war on such a huge scale. Conscription brought many problems. It removed workers from their families and jobs. It brought poor recruits into the services: the lazy, insubordinate or criminal. Ultimately, however, it was the only way to recruit personnel in large enough numbers.

⬅ **The British authorities issued National Registration cards to gather details of everyone who was eligible for conscription.**

CONSCIENTIOUS OBJECTORS

In Britain and the United States, conscription exempted people whose religious beliefs forbade them from taking part in an aggressive war. Most conscientious objectors (COs) were Quakers, Memmonites or members of other faiths that rejected violence. Many served in noncombatant positions, such as driving ambulances or working on the home front. Despite their willingness to serve, many COs experienced great prejudice. They were widely seen as being cowardly and unpatriotic. Those who refused any part in the war — usually Jehovah's Witnesses — were imprisoned.

⇒ **Conscientious objectors march against the draft in London in 1939; 'conchies' or COs had to be assessed to show that their beliefs were long held and not just a reaction to the war.**

peaked in France before the country surrendered in 1940, in Britain after the evacuation of the British Expeditionary Force from Dunkirk, and in the United States after the Japanese attack on Pearl Harbor in December 1941.

In Germany, meanwhile, young people who had been brought up with the values of the Nazi Party, volunteered to take part in what they believed was a just campaign to expand Germany's borders to encompass all Germanic peoples. For them, the Allies were aggressors who threatened legitimate German ambitions.

⇐ **This recruiting poster for the SS features an idealised blue-eyed German surrounded by Nazi insignia.**

THE BEVIN BOYS

Recruits had little choice about where they served. In Britain, that might even mean being sent to work in coal mines. The minister for labour, Ernest Bevin, was worried about maintaining coal production as so many miners had volunteered for the war. In 1943 he introduced conscription for miners. Each week his secretary drew a number – 0 to 9 – from a hat; any conscripts whose National Service number ended in that digit became a 'Bevin Boy'. Some 700,000 men served in the mines. Like conscientious objectors, they suffered prejudice: their part in the war was not officially acknowledged until 1995.

began. That was still too small to face the German army, which had been recruited by conscription since 1934. Soon the British government announced the introduction of conscription. All men aged from 18 to 41 could be called up: those aged 20 to 23 were required to sign up for the Army, Air Force or Navy.

In the United States the first draft was organized in 1940 after the fall of France. Conscriptees, who were aged 21 to 35, only had to serve for a year. That changed after Pearl Harbor: now all males aged 18 to 35 were liable to conscription, which was carried out by drawing lots within each region of the country.

Conscription

Volunteers could only do a certain amount, however. In Britain, for example, voluntary recruitment increased the size of the army to 875,000 men after the war

Ethnic Minorities

One potentially valuable source of recruitment was largely overlooked. African Americans could only serve in one of four black units, formed in 1866.

⇒ **African American volunteers join the U.S. Army Air Corps in March 1941, the first time black Americans had been allowed to join the Army Air Force – but only in black-only squadrons.**

President Roosevelt believed that forcing the Army to integrate black and white soldiers would damage morale. Black troops travelled and lived separately from their white colleagues. They even had separate medical personnel.

Nevertheless, between 367,000 and 700,000 black Americans volunteered for the military services. Usually they served in support roles, such as working on railways or in ports. Army commanders were reluctant to use them in actual conflict until later in the war. At the Battle of the Bulge in late 1944, the U.S. Army suffered a shortage of white tank crews; more than 500 African Americans volunteered and fought with distinction. Elsewhere, black volunteer pilots formed the 332nd Fighter Group – the 'Tuskegee Airmen' – which won the Presidential Unit Citation in March 1945.

Japanese Americans, meanwhile, were free to volunteer, despite the fact that many of their families were held in internment camps in the United States. A Japanese American unit fighting in Italy went on to win a disproprotionately high number of military honours.

⇧ This recruiting poster for the U.S. Navy was designed by McClelland Barclay, who had previously done illustration for magazines and Hollywood film posters.

Eyewitness

KEN RAWLINSON

Ken Rawlinson was 18 when he decided to volunteer for the British Tank Corps in 1942. At his local recruiting office, he was shown in to the office of a brigadier.

"'So you want to join the Tank Corps, laddie?" were his opening words, to which I meekly replied, "Yes Sir". Upon which he put on his peaked cap, stood up and gave me a card. "Read that aloud", he said, which I did. It turned out to be the oath of allegiance to the King. He then said, "Sign here", whereupon he gave me the King's shilling for volunteering and a railway warrant and I was "in". It took all of ten minutes…'

PHYSICAL FITNESS

One of the great challenges for all armies was to ensure that recruits were fit enough for the physical demands of soldiering. Soldiers had to be able to march long distances and carry heavy loads without becoming exhausted. Physical training (PT), together with frequent drill and exercises such as assault courses, was designed to make individuals improve their fitness quickly.

⇩ **U.S. troops perform exercises at a training ground in New York City in 1942.**

Training

It was one thing to recruit men and women in the numbers required to fight the war. It was quite another to train them to serve in a modern army.

It was not always necessary to train people for specialist jobs, of course. In all countries, recruits brought their civilian skills into the forces. The services deliberately recruited drivers as truck drivers, say, or doctors and nurses to serve in the medical corps, mechanics as ground crew for aircraft or marine engineers to work in the engine rooms of navy and merchant ships. But the sheer numbers needed meant that many people needed to learn highly specialist skills almost from scratch: there were relatively few pilots before the war broke out, for example, so air forces had to come up with ways to train their own – and as quickly as possible. One result was that, particularly early in the war, some people fighting on all sides were learning their duties on the job.

⇑ Wearing full kit and carrying rifles, members of the British Home Guard tackle an obstacle course during training in 1940; such courses were intended to improve fitness and coordination.

Basic Training

Even ordinary soldiers and sailors had to go through basic training. They were taught, for example, how to fire a rifle. Just as importantly, they were taught how to maintain it by taking it apart to clean it. Weapons could easily become jammed by dirt, so it was vital for every man to know how to keep his gun in working condition.

Firearms training could clearly be very useful. Some recruits, however, had difficulty understanding the purpose of

⇩ **This British poster reflects the danger from the accidental firing of small arms. Such accidents caused many injuries and even deaths, particularly early in the war, when new recruits were still unfamiliar with their weapons.**

DESERTION

The worst breach of discipline in any army was desertion, or running away. Soldiers had to believe that what would happen if they ran away was worse than what might happen to them if they stayed. In most armies the punishment for desertion was death. In the Soviet army deserters' families would also be punished. Men would only face the possibility of getting killed if they knew that the alternative was definitely to be killed.

MAY END LIKE THIS···

the other standard form of training: drill. Drill was carried out in platoons and usually consisted of coordinated marching and other movements, such as standing to attention or moving around one's rifle. It was repetitive and boring and required lots of concentration.

Purpose of Drill

Although it seemed to have little to do with what actually happened on the battlefield, drill had been evolved by armies over centuries precisely because it helped soldiers to fight. It had two main purposes – neither of which was particularly concerned with marching in formation. That happened rarely.

One purpose of drill was to introduce recruits to military discipline. This helped them to make the change from life as a civilian, where there was freedom to do more or less whatever he liked, to army life, where such freedom was a thing of

⟹ **This poster reflects the reputation of U.S. naval aviation training as among the most demanding in the U.S. services.**

U. S. Navy Pre Flight School

Rough, Tough, Smart

the past. It made men more accustomed to thinking of themselves as part of a group, which was essential for maintaining morale – military planners had worked out that soldiers were far more likely to fight to help their own unit than to fight for an abstract cause such as patriotism. Drill forged individuals from different backgrounds into a group, used to working together and obeying the orders of their superiors. It was also good physical training, helping to build their stamina for active duty in the field.

The other main purpose of drill was to make sure that recruits were completely familiar with sets of basic movements, such as carrying, inspecting or reloading a rifle under pressure.

ROYAL AIR FORCE

Pilots were seen as being the most glamorous of fighting men. Pilot trainees passed mental and physical tests before several weeks of flight training. During the Battle of Britain, however, some pilots went on active service after only a few hours of flying experience. They were sent off to face the enemy – and many never came back.

⟹ **RAF volunteers train as air gunners with a model aeroplane and a 'gun' with a camera inside.**

⇐ **A U.S. infantryman uses a cartoon of Adolf Hitler for bayonet practice at a training camp in Pennsylvania in the weeks after the German declaration of war on the United States in December 1941.**

GOOSE-STEP

The goose-step march of the German Army began in Prussia in the 17th century. It is an unnatural movement, so it reflects great discipline and strength. It made British writer George Orwell think of 'the vision of a boot crashing down on a face'.

What recruits complained was boring repetition would eventually make certain movements automatic so that soldiers could perform them almost in their sleep – and certainly in the dark or amid the turmoil of battle.

Discipline

All armies developed strict discipline so that soldiers would keep fighting even in the face of great danger. There were severe punishments for desertion. In the Soviet army, all units had rear detachments to intercept not only deserters but even troops retreating from the front. In all, about 158,000 Soviet troops were executed for 'desertion'.

By contrast, the United States only executed one of its 21,000 deserters during the war. The rest were tried and either imprisoned or sent back to their

⇑ **German army recruits practice the goose-step during training in 1939, before the outbreak of war. The unnatural movement was intended to demonstrate physical strength and individual discipline.**

<== British soldiers at 'battle school' practice using ropes to climb walls while their colleagues keep watch.

DISCIPLINE

It could be difficult for armies to keep order among young recruits, some of whom had been in trouble with authority in the past. In the British Army misbehaviour was dealt with by punishments ranging from compulsory parades to being confined to barracks. Military police dealt with more serious crimes, which could lead to a trial in a military court and a sentence in a military prison.

units. The exception was Eddie Slovik. Although 49 Americans were sentenced to death, Slovik was the only one whose sentence was actually carried out.

Wrong Time and Place

Slovik, a Polish-American from Detroit, had a criminal record for petty crime. Drafted and sent to France, he complained that he was too scared to fight. Eventually he gave his commanders a note that stated his intention to run away. He refused to change his mind, expecting to be sent to jail. Instead, he was shocked to be sentenced to death.

Slovik was unlucky. In winter 1944 the U.S. Army was fighting the Germans in the Ardennes and morale was low because it was clear that casualties would be high. President Eisenhower confirmed the death sentence. He noted that it was important to prevent other desertions at a difficult time. Slovik was shot by firing squad on 31 January, 1945. He is the only U.S. serviceman to have been executed for desertion since the American Civil War (1861–1865).

Eyewitness

VERNON E. GREEN

Vernon Green enrolled as a private in the U.S. 10th Infantry Regiment in 1939 and was sent for basic training.

'There was little room to err without being critiqued. Punishment was available through extra guard duty, kitchen police, policing for matchsticks and cigarette butts, marking targets on the rifle range, oral and written reprimands, and reduction in rank.'

Morale

Morale is key in order to get the best out of military forces. Asking men and women to put up with danger, boredom, discomfort and homesickness is easier if they are generally feeling confident and determined.

Morale is a positive spirit that enables a group of people or an individual to do something that otherwise they might find difficult, such as fighting a war. With good morale, people fight better because they feel positive and believe they will be victorious. With poor morale, troops may feel discouraged: they may be defeated even though victory is within their grasp.

Studies in World War I suggested that in order to face up to the physical and mental stress of conflict, men needed to be reasonably well fed and clothed, and to have reasonable shelter. They were also more likely to have good morale if they had a sense of duty and

MORALE

The French general Napoleon Bonaparte said that in war 'morale is to the physical as three is to one'. In other words, mental strength is more important even than physical strength.

PIN-UPS

A new word entered the language in 1941: the pin-up. It referred to pictures of women that military personnel cut out of magazines to stick on their walls or lockers. The women, who came to be called pin-ups too, were often film stars. Among the most famous were Betty Grable, Veronica Lake and Rita Hayworth. Most appeared first in the U.S. magazine Esquire, accompanied by a saucy poem. U.S. entertainer Bob Hope joked, 'Our American troops are ready to fight at the drop of an Esquire'.

← **Hollywood star Jane Russell admires her own picture on a plane at a U.S. Air Corps training camp in California. A group of airmen had made her their mascot.**

MEDALS

One way to maintain good morale is to reward it with medals. The highest orders for gallantry included the Victoria Cross in Britain, the Iron Cross in Germany, the Distinguished Service Cross and Medal of Honor in the United States, the Legion d'Honneur in France and the Hero of the Soviet Union.

➡ **Medals were a highly visible celebration of the courage of an individual.**

pride in their unit. The importance of this group loyalty was taken into account when structuring armies in World War II (see box, page 22). The German Wehrmacht, in particular, focused on the relationship between leaders and their men. Its soldiers were notable for their ability to keep fighting, even when forced to retreat.

Dealing with Boredom

Anyone serving in any branch of the military forces during World War II faced great danger at various times, particularly on the front line. But even when their lives were not under threat, soldiers' spirit could be undermined in other ways. One of the most harmful was boredom. Between outbreaks of fighting, there were long periods when armies and navies were not doing very much at all.

⬇ **Soldiers of the 'Berliner' Division are awarded the Iron Cross, Germany's highest order for gallantry.**

REGIMENTAL SYSTEM

Military commanders realised that the best way to get men to fight was to make them part of a small group. People might be reluctant to risk danger for an idea, like 'freedom', but they are more willing to help their friends. Armies were split into units – regiments – each with a distinctive identity, flag and traditions all designed to encourage loyalty.

MEN of VALOR
They fight for you

"When last seen he was collecting Bren and Tommy Guns and preparing a defensive position which successfully covered the withdrawal from the beach." — Excerpt from citation awarding Victoria Cross to Lt.-Col. Merritt, South Saskatchewan Regt., Dieppe, Aug. 19, 1942

⇧ **Celebrating acts of bravery, as in this Canadian poster, helped develop regimental pride and loyalty.**

Soldiers needed to be entertained and kept busy to help pass the time. They also needed to have as many home comforts as possible when they were not in the teeth of the action. Those comforts included somewhere dry to sleep, enough to eat and drink and uniforms that suited the climate and conditions. As much as possible soldiers had to be able to keep themselves and their clothes clean and dry.

The people responsible for the conditions in camp were the quartermasters. They arranged clothing, laundries, showers and bathroom facilities, food and field kitchens and horses and mules for transportation. However, for a lot of the time, soldiers would have to sleep in the open, say, or use only field rations. On the Eastern Front, the German advance into the Soviet Union in June 1941 was supplemented by food taken from local people – who were left hungry or starving as a result.

Keeping in Touch

The vast majority of recruits on all sides were serving far from home (many were overseas for the first time in their lives). They needed to keep in touch with what was happening at home – not only so that they did not worry about their families too much, but also to remind them what they were fighting for. It was vital for military personnel to know that they hadn't been forgotten by the people they were fighting for.

Writing and receiving letters was an important part of staying in contact with life at home. Army postal services made great efforts to deliver letters, even in the field. The German Army delivered post to its soldiers right up to its surrender in 1945. Meanwhile U.S. servicemen overseas received so much mail that a special system was devised to minimize the physical amount of paper being sent. In V-mail, a letter was photographed and reduced to a tiny miniature before being sent and re-enlarged at its destination.

Mental Toughness

Bravado – the attitude that 'we are better than them' – was exploited by both authorities and ordinary soldiers to boost morale. Authorities promoted stories of heroes who had achieved great feats to encourage belief among other soldiers. If individuals had an unshakable belief in their military superiority – just as Japanese troops had at the start of the war

– then it was far more likely that their morale would survive even during periods when the war was not progressing well. Soldiers with high levels of bravado were confident that things would turn back their way.

⇑ German soldiers at a victory parade in Berlin in 1940; such events encouraged public morale as well as that of the troops.

⇑ The famous shark tooth design of the Flying Tigers decorates this restored Curtiss P-40 Warhawk fighter plane.

NOSE ART

The practice of nose art – pilots painting the noses of their aircraft – began in World War I. In World War II U.S. airmen continued the tradition. The subjects varied widely. Many aircraft were pin-ups, either real or imaginary. Other popular subjects were cartoon characters such as Popeye or Micky Mouse. The U.S. unit known as the Flying Tigers, based in China, used a shark-tooth design on their fighters; the 39th Fighter Squadron in the Pacific did the same.

Entertainment

ENSA

ENSA – the Entertainments National Service Association – was formed in 1939 to entertain British service personnel. During the war it recruited stars such as the singers Gracie Fields and George Formby and the actors Laurence Olivier and Ralph Richardson, who produced Shakespeare plays for the military in Europe. Many performers were not so eminent, however – there were not enough stars to go around. The poor quality of some of the so-called entertainment was summed up in ENSA's popular nickname: Every Night Something Awful.

Key to maintaining morale was preventing personnel on active duty from becoming bored. One way was to make sure there was ample entertainment.

That might take the form of regular showings of films or of theatrical performances. There was no shortage of professional or amateur performers willing to offer their services. Performers even toured bases near the front lines, entertaining troops on active duty. In 1996 the U.S. singer and comedian Bob Hope was named an 'honorary veteran of the U.S. armed services' for his constant touring schedule (he continued to entertain U.S. troops overseas for some 50 years). There was also a ready supply of volunteers from within the ranks themselves. Many units formed 'concert parties', in which a few musicians, singers or comedians might put on an evening's entertainment for their fellow servicemen.

⇒ **U.S. comedian Bob Hope entertains injured GIs at a military hospital in New Caledonia in the Pacific Ocean during a tour in 1944.**

⇒ **British troops are entertained by a boxing match between two champions specially staged at a training camp in 1939.**

GLENN MILLER

'Big bands' became popular in the 1930s, playing jazz and swing music. In 1944, one of the leading stars, Glenn Miller, formed the 50-piece U.S. Army Air Force Band, to entertain service personnel in the United States and Britain. The band played some 800 performances and even recorded broadcasts in German, intended to help demoralize enemy soldiers who wanted to listen to Miller's dance music.

⇐ **Glenn Miller (in hat) boarded a flight to France in December 1944, but the plane never reached its destination.**

The USO

For U.S. troops, entertainment was organized by the United Services Organization (USO; see box, page 29). The USO had been established in early 1941, when President Roosevelt asked his officials to set up an organization to look after the spiritual and recreational needs of U.S. service personnel.

Among the other activities it arranged through its 3,000 bases around the world, the USO organized famous 'camp shows' in which professional entertainers or film stars visited military bases to perform. Through some 300,000 performances, the USO entertained about 160 million servicemen and women. A contemporary article in *Look* magazine noted, 'For the little time the show lasts, the men are taken straight to the familiar Main Street that is the goal of every fighting American far away from home.'

The USO also organized dances where servicemen could dance with female volunteers, movie shows and canteens that provided free coffee and doughnuts. There were also quiet rooms to relax, read or write letters home. The British equivalent, ENSA (see box, page 24), was less ambitious, concentrating on providing entertainment – not always of the highest quality.

Music and Morale

Music was almost universally popular. Forces' radio stations were set up by virtually all combatant countries in order to provide military personnel with

Eyewitness

HARRY SHARPLES

Harry Sharples was a welder in the Royal Navy who served in the Mediterranean, the Indian Ocean and the Pacific.

'We had entertainment on board the ship. When we were in the Pacific, they used to come into the hangers and give us a show. We'd be all drinking or having limejuice to keep us cool. We had quite a lot of entertainers. They would fly out to us. We used to swap films with the Americans because we had like a cinema in the hanger sometimes.'

entertainment and information. Soldiers far from home found familiar voices and familiar tunes reassuring. Some of the most popular songs of the time were sentimental or nostalgic, drawing on the universal wish for a return to a more peaceful time (see box, right). Vera Lynn, known in her native Britain as the 'forces' sweetheart', had a huge hit with a wistful yet positive song: 'We'll meet again'. The song urged listeners to 'Keep smiling through' and promised 'I know we'll meet again some sunny day'.

Other songs mocked the enemy or poked fun at army life, including songs such as 'Der Fuehrer's Face' or 'Praise the Lord and Pass the Ammunition'. Irving Berlin's popular song 'God Bless America' was actually written a few years before the war but it came to be seen as a kind of alternative national anthem. Like Bob Hope, Berlin was constantly on tour entertaining the troops. He was particularly popular for his performances of a song he had actually written about soldier life during World War I, 'Oh How I Hate to Get Up in the Morning'.

Music and Dances

Music was essential for dances, which were popular, particularly because they usually involved interaction with women working in the various arms of the services. Off-duty, soldiers in Britain or the United States found it easy to find dance partners, while German officers in occupied France enjoyed socializing with French women (many of whom would be punished for this by their countrymen after the war).

NOSTALGIC SONGS

Popular songs were often sentimental. At a time when families were separated, they reminded everyone of better times. The German love song 'Lili Marlene', about a soldier parted from his girlfriend, became hugely popular among Axis forces in Europe, because it was widely broadcast on the German forces radio station, Radio Belgrade. Its sentiments were also popular among the enemy, who secretly listened in to hear the familiar tune.

⬆ The 1939 novelty song '(We're Gonna Hang Out) the Washing on the Siegfried Line' predicted a swift Allied victory over Germany's defensive line.

27

The most popular form of music for dancing was known as swing, which had evolved from jazz in the United States over the previous two decades. The Nazis had condemned jazz as inferior music, but even German troops secretly listened

> " *There'll be bluebirds over the white cliffs of Dover tomorrow, just you wait and see.* "
>
> 'WHITE CLIFFS OF DOVER', VERA LYNN

to broadcasts of artists such as Glenn Miller or other swing bands, whose up-tempo music was perfect for dancing.

Other popular performers included the Andrews Sisters: Laverne, Maxene and Patty. This singing trio were known as the

HUMOUR

Humour was vital to morale. Many of those on active service developed a sense of humour that was often quite dark in its tone. It was based on shared suffering and the possibility of death.

'sweethearts of the Armed Forces Radio Service', for which they made many appearances. They also toured widely to military bases, and recorded special 'V-records' that were only distributed to members of the armed services. The sisters helped found the Hollywood Canteen, in Los Angeles, California.

GI NEWSPAPERS

For a picture of the progress of the war, U.S. personnel turned to **The Stars and Stripes**. *Founded during the American Civil War, the newspaper was an independent source of information for the services. The reporters often worked close to the front line and GIs trusted that they were reporting the news from the soldiers' point of view, not from that of the government.*

⇒ *Stars and Stripes reports on the celebrations for Victory in Europe (VE) Day, 8 May, 1945.*

THE STARS AND STRIPES
MEDITERRANEAN

Vol. 2, No. 155, Wednesday, May 9, 1945   ITALY EDITION * * TWO LIRE

BIG 3 HAILS VE-DAY; JAPS NEXT-TRUMAN

N.Y.C. Goes Joy Crazy On Victory

By Sgt. MILTON LEHMAN
(Stars and Stripes Staff Writer)
NEW YORK, May 7 (Delayed)—The Big Town greeted the news of the war's end in Europe today as was expected it would — it went crazy with joy.

Newsstands were besieged from 9 AM and dealers were selling as fast as they could make change. Such headlines as "Nazis Quit," in white letters on black in the New York Post; "Nazis Give Up, Surrender to Allies and Russia announced" in the World Telegram; "It's VE-Day (in black), Last German Units Yield (in red letters), and "Remember Pearl Harbor," (white letters on black) in the New York Journal-American.

Over the radio, which supplied the best running account of news developments, commentators were on hand early to give the account of surrender from what news was available, minute by minute.

One New York radio spokesman observed that the world had been expecting this news. Another said, "ad libbing when his prepared script ran out, "whenever big things happen, New Yorkers always want to throw things down from the window."

Toward Times ...

Big Four Attitude Assures Parley's Success--Molotov

SAN FRANCISCO, May 8 (ANS) —Agreement among the Big Four on what amendments to the Dumbarton Oaks proposals shall be sponsored by the U. S., Britain, Russia and China is so complete, V. M. Molotov announced today, that success of the world security organization meetings here is virtually assured.

Big Four discussions on amendments are at an end, he said at a press conference yesterday, adding that he hopes the work of the United Nations conference will be ...

VE-Day Ceremony At Caserta Today

AFHQ, May 8 — A VE-Day ceremony will be held tomorrow for American and British servicemen at 10 AM in the Royal Palace Grounds at Caserta, it was announced today.

It was announced that hours for curfew and bars will not be extended.

War's Official End Today, 0001 Hours

The war against Germany ended officially at 0001 hours today under the surrender terms signed at 0241 hours Monday.

The victory in Europe was proclaimed yesterday in broadcasts to their peoples and their Allies of all the United Nations by President Harry S. Truman, Prime Minister Winston S. Churchill and Marshal Joseph V. Stalin.

The order to cease fire was given to German forces on land, sea and air on Monday, but resistance continued on a few scattered fronts of the European continent where the costliest war of all time had raged for more than five years and eight months.

Mr. Truman declared that this "is a solemn but glorious hour." He said that "his only wish is that Franklin D. Roosevelt had lived to witness this day."

"The flags of freedom fly all over Europe," the President said. But he told the country ... was half over. He warned the Japanese nothing but complete destruction ... render unconditionally.

Mr. T...

PRESIDENT TRUMAN   GENERAL EISENHOWER

USO

The U.S. United Services Organization (USO) was famous for offering servicemen and women a 'home away from home'. Even though they might be far from the United States, they could spend their leave in more than 3,000 clubs.

⇒ **Servicemen chat and pen letters home in a 'writing room' in a USO club.**

Set up by showbusiness stars, the Hollywood Canteen offered free food and entertainment to anyone in uniform – along with the chance to be waited on by a famous volunteer such as movie star Betty Grable.

At the Pictures

The 1930s and 1940s were the heyday of Hollywood. During the war, audiences at home flocked to the cinema; British and American soldiers were just as enthusiastic. Many film stars had volunteered, but Hollywood continued to produce films. Many were used as a subtle form of propaganda that depicted a far more harmonious version of American society than actually existed at home. In Britain, films such as *Mrs. Miniver* (1942) also promoted a sentimental view of the country. In the same way, German films showed examples of German bravery, while Russian movies referred back to nationalist heroes from history.

⇓ **Wearing coats and hats to protect them against a downpour, U.S. troops watch their nightly movie on the island of Guadalcanal in the Pacific.**

Few films went beyond a simplistic view of the conflict. One that did was *Casablanca* (1942), starring Humphrey Bogart as a bar owner in Morocco, which was occupied by the Vichy French. Through an old girlfriend who is now married to a resistance leader, Bogart's character is forced to face up to complex moral dilemmas about the war.

Medical Care

Medical care did not only involve looking after the wounded. It was important to protect fighting men from illness and from psychological problems such as depression.

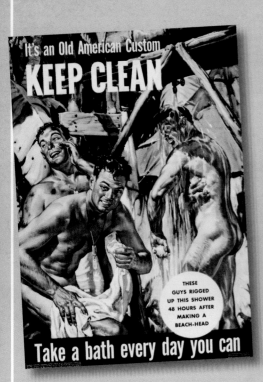

It's an Old American Custom

KEEP CLEAN

THESE GUYS RIGGED UP THIS SHOWER 48 HOURS AFTER MAKING A BEACH-HEAD

Take a bath every day you can

⇧ This U.S. War Department poster urged soldiers to keep as clean as possible: it was vital to avoid losing soldiers due to illness or infection.

The best way to keep healthy was not to get sick in the first place. People going overseas were vaccinated against infection or took malaria tablets. In Asia and Africa, in particular, insects such as mosquitos carried potentially harmful diseases. Soldiers were also encouraged to keep themselves as clean as possible: some took baths or showers more frequently than they had at home during peacetime. In the same way, they often ate better than they had before. Services food was planned to be as nutritious as possible – although it was also usually very plain and repetitive.

Elements of Good Health

In the field, all countries' medical services had to cope with sickness as well as with battlefield injuries. Psychological problems were also common in the traumatic situation of wartime.

⇒ A recruiting poster for the American Red Cross. During the war, the Red Cross enrolled more than 104,000 nurses for military service and began a national programme to collect blood for wounded soldiers.

BATTLEFIELD INJURIES

Most battlefield injuries were caused by gunshots or explosions. Surgeons were helped by new drugs that prevented infection and by the availability of large amounts of blood for transfusions. The war saw the start of modern blood transfusion services.

THE RED CROSS

The Red Cross operated widely in Europe in World War II. It tried to find people who had fled or been moved away from bombing or fighting and had lost touch with their families. The Red Cross also helped prisoners of war, arranging postal services and letting families know where the prisoners were. The Red Cross was allowed to inspect war prisons under the Geneva Convention, which laid down rules of warfare. Because Japan and the Soviet Union were not signed up to the convention, the Red Cross had less impact in those countries.

Good health care was not simply a matter of physical well-being. It was widely recognized that it was vital to troop morale. It was unavoidable that people would fall sick or get wounded – so personnel had to be confident that they would be looked after if that happened.

Combat Medics

Battlefield medical care depended on having trained personnel as close to the front line as possible and on evacuating the wounded as quickly as possible. In general, a patient was only removed as far from the front line as his or her injury required for treatment and recovery.

Immediate medical care was usually provided at the front line by a combat

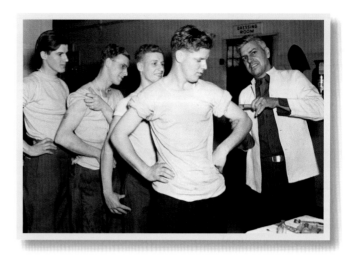

❝At the front [soldiers] called you 'medic' and before you knew it, it was 'Doc'.

BUDDY GIANELLONI, U.S. COMBAT MEDIC

medic, a soldier trained in first aid and trauma care. Combat medics – called corpsmen in the U.S. Navy and Marines – lived alongside the combat troops. They wore a prominent red cross to identify themselves as medical personnel, so the enemy did not attack them. Still, many were killed as they worked under fire to get the wounded out of harm's way.

Combat medics were trained to check and clean wounds, inject morphine as a painkiller and apply tourniquets and bandages. Combat medics were also responsible for the general welfare of

⇐ A U.S. poster calls for nursing recruits for the Civilian Defense Volunteer Office. Members of the largest women's auxiliary organisation, the American Women's Voluntary Services, were also trained in emergency medical care.

⇐ The four Benditt brothers, who all joined the U.S. Army on the same day in 1943, wait to receive inoculations against common contagious diseases at Fort Eustis, Virginia.

their unit, including looking after men who became sick.

Many medics were conscientious objectors whose religious faith did not allow them to fight an aggressive war. They sometimes aroused suspicion and hostility from combat troops – until they witnessed the medics' bravery under fire.

Chain of Evacuation

The next level of medical care was provided by mobile field hospitals and evacuation centres. Casualties were moved on jeeps fitted with stretcher carriers, by truck or by stretcher bearers. The field hospital was staffed by some 60 men, a half dozen nurses and a half dozen surgeons. It concentrated on wounds to the chest, abdomen and upper legs.

The more seriously wounded could be evacuated by rail or by air (often on aircraft that had flown in medical supplies). In the U.S. Army, the system was known as the 'chain of evacuation'. First tried during Operation Torch, the Allied invasion of North Africa in November 1942, it was later widely applied throughout U.S. military services. Patients who were unable to be treated in military hospitals were moved to general hospitals in the United States or areas far from the fighting.

PENICILLIN

In 1928 Scottish scientist Alexander Fleming discovered penicillin, a mould that killed bacteria. The war boosted research into the drug. Teams in England and the United States learned to produce it in large quantities: some 2.3 million doses by D-Day in June 1944. The drug greatly improved the chances of wounded soldiers in Europe and the Pacific in the last year of the war. It helped prevent their wounds becoming infected.

⇒ U.S. medics administer an emergency blood transfusion in a field hospital in the Pacific.

⇐ **U.S. corpsmen in Italy in 1944 load an army mule with supplies of blood plasma, used for transfusions, to be transported to a forward medical aid station.**

The system of evacuation was so effective – alongside the development of penicillin – that in World War II only four per cent of wounded Americans who were admitted to hospital died; in World War I that proportion had been eight per cent, while in the American Civil War it had been closer to 50 per cent.

Eyewitness

JOY TRINDLES

Joy Trindles was a British nurse. She landed in Normandy shortly after the first Allied troops on D-Day in June 1944.

'We landed and were sniped at by Germans. One of our doctors was killed and an orderly was shot and we had to amputate his leg at the side of the road. We had to be careful because everywhere was mined. Notices were on the roadsides. Lots of dead bodies.'

Psychological Health

One of the focuses of medical care was on the emotional trauma that was inevitable given the constant danger and stress of active service. As much as possible, mental casualties were dealt with at the front line. That was a great change from World War I. In that conflict, people suffering from what was known at the time as 'shell shock' were often regarded as cowards who were seeking to avoid duty. Many shell-shocked soldiers were executed for desertion.

By World War II, medical authorities increasingly recognized that stress was a medical condition that sufferers could not prevent. One in 12 of all American patients suffered from psychological problems: more than 400,000 of them had to be sent home.

Nurses' care for the morale of the wounded was supported by the efforts of service chaplains. Voluntary organisations such as the Red Cross and the Salvation Army also ran programmes to maintain the spirits of sick or recuperating patients.

CARE OF THE WOUNDED

Huge numbers of people were wounded in the war: 4.6 million in Germany, 18 million in the Soviet Union, 300,000 each for Britain and the United States. Some were not seriously injured, but many infantry had suffered severe bullet wounds; pilots, tank crew or sailors frequently suffered severe burns; many men in all services lost limbs in explosions. As a consequence of the war, there were great advances in plastic surgery to repair burns, as pioneered by the surgeon Sir Harold Gillies in the United Kingdom. A similar step forward came in prosthetics for amputees. The U.S. Army Prosthetic Research Lab (APRL) developed a hook operated by the muscles of the bicep that is still used today as a replacement hand.

Nursing Corps

Lessons from World War I were applied in nursing, too. Matrons and other senior nurses had served in the earlier war. They had learned the importance of caring for patients' spiritual well-being and morale, as well as their physical health.

All armed forces recruited huge numbers of nurses. Nursing was one of the main opportunities for military service open to women. There were many volunteers. On the day the Japanese bombed Pearl Harbor, there were 1,000 nurses in the U.S. Army Nurse Corps. In the next four years, 59,000 nurses served. In Britain, the Queen Alexandra's Imperial Military Nursing Service also expanded rapidly. In 1941 British military nurses were given a new system of rank as a sign that they would be seen as military personnel first, and nurses second.

⇑ **Wounded GIs exercise during a rehabilitation programme at a hotel converted to a general hospital in Palm Beach, Florida, in April 1944.**

Demobilisation

Once the fighting was over, everyone wanted to get home. This process was known as demobilisation – and it was just as huge an undertaking as the original mobilisation had been.

The United States had 12 million service personnel overseas at the end of the war. The British had 5 million men and women in uniform. Many Soviet soldiers were not demobilised, but simply redirected to other duties. The German and Japanese militaries were destroyed. After being released from captivity their soldiers were left to get themselves home. Large numbers failed to make it.

A Sensitive Task

The challenge for authorities was not only to get the soldiers home. An even bigger potential problem was helping them to return to civilian life. Some had been away from home for years.

⇨ **U.S. veterans crowd the decks of the *Queen Elizabeth* as it brings them into New York harbour at the end of the war.**

CIVVY STREET

During the war, a gap opened between those in service and those at home. There was suspicion between the two groups. Soldiers saw some civilians as having made money from the war. That made it even harder for some veterans to adjust to civilian life.

Some government planners were concerned that the sheer number of people arriving home would cause social and economic problems: there were simply not enough jobs to go around. Others, particularly in the United States, worried that too rapid a demobilisation would leave the country weakened. That was a concern now that ideological differences with the Soviet Union were already threatening to put the former allies into opposition. On the other hand, individual servicemen and women were impatient to get home as soon as possible. Rioting broke out among some U.S. personnel in the Pacific theatre who were frustrated at the slowness of the process.

Planning Ahead

Planning for demobilisation was so complicated that it actually began two years before the defeat of Germany, by which time an eventual Allied victory was all but certain. There were all sorts of considerations to take into account. One was the length of service. It was naturally fair that those people who had served longest should be demobilized first. But

⇑ **A British soldier returns home at the end of the war. For some returning troops, coming home was an anticlimax.**

there were some people whose skills were more urgently needed in civilian life to help begin the economic recovery – they had to be returned to the workforce quickly. Meanwhile, soldiers needed to be paid – some had not received their pay for a considerable length of time.

Continuing Service

In addition, the Allies could not demobilise all of their soldiers. Large numbers of servicemen remained in Germany to maintain order and to oversee the country's return to peace. In Japan, General Douglas MacArthur led an occupying force of 350,000 Americans who would effectively govern the country for seven years. In Britain, meanwhile,

Eyewitness

JOHN RAWLINGS

British infantry officer John Rawlings was demobilised in Germany in 1945 and made his way home across the Channel.

'I received my officers' demob document which I still have. Throughout my six years service my conduct was stated as "exemplary". This is a word I had not met before and I took the first opportunity to check in a dictionary and was pleased to find it was complimentary.'

GI BILL OF RIGHTS

The Servicemen's Readjustment Act, or GI Bill, became law in June 1944. It would change the shape of the United States. For one thing, it entitled servicemen to a no-interest loan to buy a house: some 2.4 million people moved home. Another provision gave servicemen a grant of $20 a week for a year while they looked for a job. Perhaps the most influential clause allowed any war veteran to enter higher education. Just over half of them – 7.8 million people – had studied in higher-education by the time the scheme ended in 1956. That changed the economy because the additional education produced specialists in a wide range of areas, such as technology.

Facing Problems

Demobilisation was often not easy. After the initial joy of returning home, there was often stress about finding work and money. Some men also found it difficult to fit back into family life. Wives and children had become used to their absence. In many cases women had grown accustomed to going out to work for themselves. They did not necessarily want to go back to being housewives. Around the world, the end of hostilities marked the beginning of new problems, which ensured that the impact of the war would continue to be felt on an emotional level long after the final shots.

the demand for military personnel was so high that national service – a programme of compulsory enrollment in the services for young men – remained in place for 15 years after the end of the war.

The British had had experience with large-scale demobilisation after World War I. They followed the lessons they had learned then. The United States, whose involvment in the earlier war had involved far fewer men, did not have any such pattern to follow. That was another reason that U.S. demobilisation provoked more dissatisfaction than in the United Kingdom. The great lesson the British had learned was that demobilisation had to be transparently fair, so that those whose demobilisation was delayed understood precisely the reasons why others were released first.

> *…the best money that can be spent for the welfare of the nation…*
> SENATE FINANCE COMMITTEE, ON GI BILL

⟹ **U.S. staff sergeant Edwin S. Williams meets his young daughter Patricia for the first time on his return home to St. Louis, Missouri, in October 1945.**

Timeline of
World War II

1939

SEPTEMBER:
German troops invade and overrun Poland
Britain and France declare war on Germany
The Soviet Union invades eastern Poland and extends control to the Baltic states
The Battle of the Atlantic begins
NOVEMBER:
The Soviet Union launches a winter offensive against Finland

1940

APRIL:
Germany invades Denmark and Norway
Allied troops land in Norway
MAY:
Germany invades Luxembourg, the Netherlands, Belgium and France
Allied troops are evacuated at Dunkirk
JUNE:
Italy declares war on France and Britain
German troops enter Paris
France signs an armistice with Germany
Italy bombs Malta in the Mediterranean
JULY:
German U-boats inflict heavy losses on Allied convoys in the Atlantic
Britain sends warships to neutralise the French fleet in North Africa
The Battle of Britain begins
SEPTEMBER:
Luftwaffe air raids begin the Blitz – the bombing of London and other British cities
Italian troops advance from Libya into Egypt
Germany, Italy and Japan sign the Tripartite Pact
OCTOBER:
Italy invades Greece; Greek forces, aided by the British, mount a counterattack
DECEMBER:
British troops at Sidi Barrani, Egypt, force the Italians to retreat

1941

JANUARY:
Allied units capture Tobruk in Libya
British forces in Sudan attack Italian East Africa
FEBRUARY:
Allies defeat Italy at Benghazi, Libya
Rommel's Afrika Korps arrive in Tripoli
MARCH:
The Africa Korps drive British troops back from El Agheila
APRIL:
German, Italian and Hungarian units invade Yugoslavia
German forces invade Greece
The Afrika Korps beseige Tobruk
MAY:
The British sink the German battleship *Bismarck*
JUNE:
German troops invade the Soviet Union
JULY:
German forces advance to within 16 kilometres (10 miles) of Kiev
AUGUST:
The United States bans the export of oil to Japan
SEPTEMBER:
German forces start the siege of Leningrad
German Army Group Centre advances on Moscow
NOVEMBER:
British troops begin an attack to relieve Tobruk
The Allies liberate Ethiopia
DECEMBER:
Japanese aircraft attack the U.S. Pacific Fleet at Pearl Harbor
Japan declares war on the United States and Britain
The United States, Britain and the Free French declare war on Japan
Japanese forces invade the Philippines, Malaya and Thailand, and defeat the British garrison in Hong Kong

1942

JANUARY:
Japan attacks the Dutch East Indies and invades Burma
Rommel launches a new offensive in Libya

FEBRUARY:

Singapore surrenders to the Japanese

APRIL:

The Bataan Peninsula in the Philippines falls to the Japanese

MAY:

U.S. and Japanese fleets clash at the Battle of the Coral Sea

Rommel attacks the Gazala Line in Libya

JUNE:

The U.S. Navy defeats the Japanese at the Battle of Midway

Rommel recaptures Tobruk and the Allies retreat to Egypt

JULY:

The Germans take Sebastopol after a long siege and advance into the Caucasus

AUGUST:

U.S. Marines encounter fierce Japanese resistance in the Solomons

SEPTEMBER–OCTOBER:

Allied forces defeat Axis troops at El Alamein, Egypt – the first major Allied victory of the war

NOVEMBER:

U.S. and British troops land in Morocco and Algeria

1943

FEBRUARY:

The German Sixth Army surrenders at Stalingrad

The Japanese evacuate troops from Guadalcanal in the Solomons

MAY:

Axis forces in Tunisia surrender, ending the campaign in North Africa

JULY:

U.S. troops make landings on New Georgia Island in the Solomons

The Red Army wins the Battle of Kursk

Allied troops land on Sicily

British bombers conduct massive raids on Hamburg

AUGUST:

German forces occupy Italy

SEPTEMBER:

Allied units begin landings on mainland Italy

Italy surrenders, prompting a German invasion of northern Italy

OCTOBER:

The Red Army liberates the Caucasus

NOVEMBER:

U.S. carrier aircraft attack Rabaul in the Solomons

1944

JANUARY:

The German siege of Leningrad ends

FEBRUARY:

U.S. forces conquer the Marshall Islands

MARCH:

The Soviet offensive reaches the Dniester River

Allied aircraft bomb the monastery at Monte Cassino in Italy

JUNE:

U.S. troops enter the city of Rome

D-Day–the Allies begin the invasion of northern Europe

U.S. aircraft defeat the Japanese fleet at the Battle of the Philippine Sea

JULY:

The Red Army begins its offensive to clear the Baltic states

Soviet tanks enter Poland

AUGUST:

Japanese troops withdraw from Myitkyina in Burma

French forces liberate Paris

Allied units liberate towns in France, Belgium and the Netherlands

OCTOBER:

Soviet and Yugoslavian troops capture Belgrade, the Yugoslav capital

The Japanese suffer defeat at the Battle of Leyte Gulf

DECEMBER:

Hitler counterattacks in the Ardennes in the Battle of the Bulge

1945

JANUARY:

The U.S. Army lands on Luzon in the Philippines

The Red Army liberates Auschwitz

Most of Poland and Czechoslovakia are liberated by the Allies

FEBRUARY:

U.S. troops take the Philippine capital, Manila

U.S. Marines land on the island of Iwo Jima

Soviet troops strike west across Germany

The U.S. Army heads towards the River Rhine

APRIL:

U.S. troops land on the island of Okinawa

Mussolini is shot by partisans

Soviet troops assault Berlin

Hitler commits suicide in his bunker

MAY:

All active German forces surrender

JUNE:

Japanese resistance ends in Burma and on Okinawa

AUGUST:

Atomic bombs are dropped on Hiroshima and Nagasaki

Japan surrenders

World War II: Europe

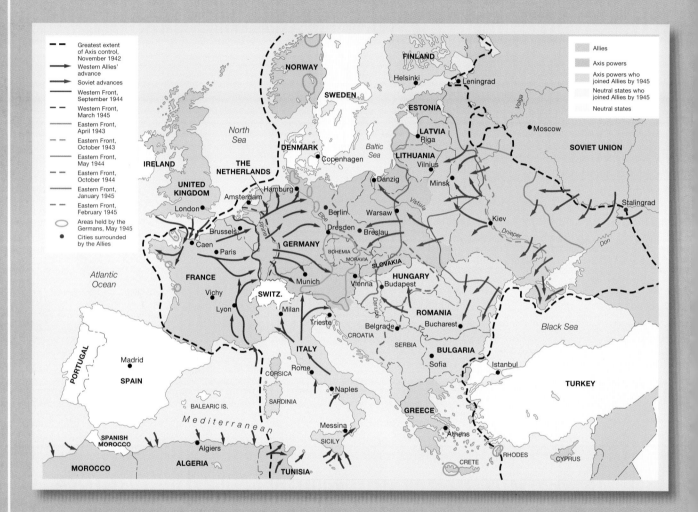

Map legend:
- Greatest extent of Axis control, November 1942
- Western Allies' advance
- Soviet advances
- Western Front, September 1944
- Western Front, March 1945
- Eastern Front, April 1943
- Eastern Front, October 1943
- Eastern Front, May 1944
- Eastern Front, October 1944
- Eastern Front, January 1945
- Eastern Front, February 1945
- Areas held by the Germans, May 1945
- Cities surrounded by the Allies

- Allies
- Axis powers
- Axis powers who joined Allies by 1945
- Neutral states who joined Allies by 1945
- Neutral states

The war began with rapid German advances through the Low Countries and northern France. In June 1941 German armies struck through eastern Europe into the Soviet Union, besieging Leningrad and Stalingrad. However, Allied landings in North Africa led to eventual victory there and opened the way for the invasion of Sicily and then of the Italian peninsula itself, forcing Italy to surrender. In the east the defeat of the German Sixth Army at Stalingrad

forced a long retreat during which German forces were harried by communist guerrillas at all moments. In June 1944 Allied forces landed in northern France on D-Day and began to fight their way towards Berlin. As the Soviet advance closed in and the Americans and British crossed the Rhine River into Germany, defeat became inevitable. Hitler committed suicide in his bunker at the heart of his failed Reich, or empire.

World War II: The Pacific

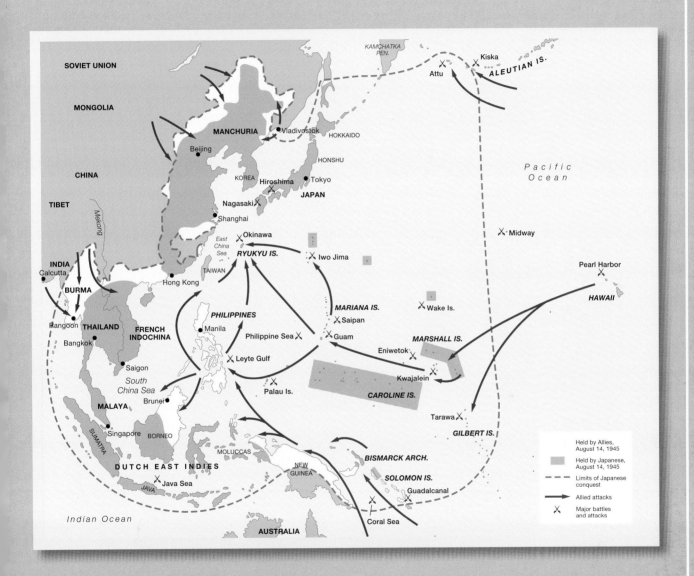

The Pacific conflict began with swift Japanese advances and occupation of territory throughout Southeast Asia, Malaya, the East Indies, the Philippines and the island groups of the Pacific. The U.S. fleet was weakened by the attack on Pearl Harbor, but the damage it suffered was repaired remarkably quickly. After the naval victory at Midway in June 1942, U.S. commanders fought a campaign of 'island hopping', overcoming strong local Japanese resistance to establish a series of stepping stones that would bring their bombers close enough to attack the Japanese home islands. Meanwhile, British and Indian troops pushed back the Japanese advance from Burma.

Biographies

Neville Chamberlain

British statesman. Conservative prime minister from 1937 to 1940, Chamberlain led the policy of appeasement of Hitler. He argued that giving in to Hitler's demands was the best way to prevent war. When the policy failed, he resigned in favour of Winston Churchill.

Churchill, Winston

British statesman. Churchill became British prime minister in May 1940 after a controversial political career. He was an energetic, inspiring and imaginative leader. His powerful speeches and his careful cultivation of Britain's U.S. allies were vital to the Allies' war effort. After the war's end Churchill was defeated in a general election, but he later became prime minister again in 1951.

De Gaulle, Charles

French statesman. French army officer De Gaulle escaped to London after the German invasion of France in 1939 and set up the Free French to oppose the Vichy regime's collaboration with Germany. Under De Gaulle's leadership, the Free French grew to include some 300,000 fighters, including partisans of the French Resistance. In 1945 he was elected president of France and later founded the Fifth Republic.

Eisenhower, Dwight D.

U.S. general. Eisenhower was part of the U.S. war plans division when he was promoted in June 1942 to become commander of U.S. forces in Europe. He led the Allied landings in North Africa and Sicily and the capture of Rome. As supreme commander of Allied forces, he led the D-Day landings in northern France and the liberation of Paris and advance into Germany. His popularity was reflected by his election in 1952 as the 34th president of the United States, a position he held for 12 years.

Goebbels, Joseph

Nazi leader. Joseph Goebbels was the head of Nazi Party propaganda and later became minister of propaganda in the Nazi government. He used mass media and cinema skilfully to promote Nazi views. At the end of the war, he killed his children and committed suicide with his wife.

Hirohito

Emperor of Japan. Hirohito reluctantly approved the growth of army power and the militarization of Japanese society. He also backed the aggressive foreign policy that eventually led to war, but in 1945 he supported the leaders who wanted to surrender unconditionally. After the war he gave up his divine status and became a constitutional monarch.

Hitler, Adolf

Dictator of Germany. After serving as a soldier in World War I, Adolf Hitler joined a minor political party that he renamed the National Socialist Workers' Party (Nazis). Hitler was elected as chancellor of Germany in 1933 and became leader (Führer) in 1934. His policies were based on anti-Semitism and anti-communism, militarism and the aggressive expansion of Germany. His invasion of Poland in September 1939 sparked the outbreak of the war. Hitler's war leadership was erratic and contributed to Germany's eventual defeat; Hitler himself committed suicide in his bunker in Berlin in the last days of the war.

Hope, Bob

U.S. entertainer. Comedian and singer Bob Hope was one of the biggest movie stars at the start of the war. He became famous for his constant tours of U.S. overseas bases to put on shows for service personnel. Having performed similar tours in later wars in Korea, Vietnam and the Persian Gulf, Hope was acknowledged in 1997 by the U.S. Congress as the first 'Honorary Veteran' in U.S. history.

MacArthur, Douglas

U.S. general. A veteran of World War I, MacArthur commanded the defence of the Philippines against Japan in 1941 before becoming supreme Allied commander in the Southwest Pacific. He commanded the U.S. attacks on New Guinea and the Philippines. After the end of the war, he became supreme Allied commander of Japan and oversaw the country's rapid postwar recovery.

Miller, Dorrie

Miller was an African-American seaman who served at Pearl Harbor in December 1941. Although at the time African Americans were only allowed to serve as orderlies, his courage during the Japanese attack earned him the Navy Cross and made him a national hero.

Montgomery, Bernard

British field marshal. Montgomery led the British Eighth Army in North Africa, where it defeated Rommel's Afrika Korps, and then shared joint command of the invasion of Sicily and Italy. He collaborated with U.S. general Eisenhower on planning the D-Day landings in France, where he commanded all land forces; Montgomery went on to command an army group in the advance toward Germany, where he eventually received the German surrender.

Mussolini, Benito

Italian dictator. Mussolini came to power in Italy in 1922 promoting fascism, a political philosophy based on a militaristic form of nationalism. He led attempts to re-create an Italian empire with overseas conquests. Mussolini became Hitler's ally in 1936 and entered the war on the Nazis' side. Italian campaigns went badly in the Balkans and North Africa, however. When the Allies invaded Italy in 1943 Mussolini was sacked by the king; he became president of a puppet German republic in northern Italy. He was executed by Italian partisan fighters at the end of the war.

Rommel, Erwin

German field marshal. Rommel was a tank commander who led the Afrika Korps in North Africa and later led the defence of northern France against the Allied invasion. When he was discovered to be part of a plot to assassinate Adolf Hitler, he was forced to commit suicide.

Roosevelt, Franklin D.

U.S. president. Democrat politician Franklin Delano Roosevelt enjoyed a privileged upbringing before entering politics and becoming governor of New York. He first came to power as president in 1932, when he was elected to apply his New Deal to solve the worst problems of the Great Depression. Reelected in 1936 and again in 1940 he fully supported the Allies, offering supplies to help fight the Germans. He was reelected in 1944, the only president to be elected for four terms, but died in office shortly before the end of the war against Japan.

Rosie the Riveter

A fictional American worker who first appeared in a popular song but whose image then appeared on posters and stamps to encourage women to take industrial jobs during the war. The various depictions of Rosie were based on a number of specific individual workers.

Stalin, Joseph

Soviet dictator. Stalin was a Bolshevik from Georgia who rose to prominence for his skill as an administrator. In 1922 he became general secretary of the Communist Party of the Soviet Union founded by Lenin. Stalin introduced programs to encourage agriculture and industry and in the 1930s got rid of many thousands of potential enemies in purges, having them jailed or executed. Having made a pact with Hitler in 1939, he was surprised when Hitler invaded the Soviet Union in 1941 but rallied the Red Army to eventual victory. At the end of the war, he imposed Soviet rule on eastern Europe.

Yamamoto, Isoroko

Japanese admiral. Yamamoto was a visionary naval planner who planned Japan's attack on the U.S. base at Pearl Harbor and its early Pacific campaigns. He was killed when the Americans shot down his aircraft in 1943, alerted by decoded Japanese radio communications.

Glossary

Allies One of the two groups of combatants in the war. The main Allies were Britain, the Soviet Union, the United States, British Empire troops, and free forces from occupied nations.

antibiotic A medicine that can halt the spread of infection.

anti-Semitism A hatred of Jews and Judaism.

armistice A temporary halt in fighting agreed to by both sides.

armour A term referring to armoured vehicles, such as tanks.

artillery Large weapons such as big guns and howitzers.

Aryan In Nazi propaganda, relating to a mythical master race of Nordic peoples.

Axis One of the two groups of combatants in the war. The leading Axis powers were Germany, Italy, and Japan.

blitzkrieg A German word meaning "lightning war." It referred to the tactic of rapid land advance supported by great airpower.

Bolsheviks Members of the Communist Party that took power in Russia after the 1917 Revolution.

casualty Someone who is killed or wounded in conflict, or who is missing but probably dead.

collaborator Someone who works with members of enemy forces who are occupying his or her country.

communism A political philosophy based on state control of the economy and distribution of wealth, followed in the Soviet Union from 1917 and in China from 1948.

corps A military formation smaller than an army, made up of a number of divisions operating together under a general.

counteroffensive A set of attacks that defend against enemy attacks.

empire A number of countries governed by a single country.

embargo An order to temporarily stop something, especially trading.

espionage The use of spies or secret agents to obtain information about the plans of a foreign government.

evacuation The act of moving someone from danger to a safe position.

Fascism A political philosophy promoted by Mussolini in Italy based on dictatorial leadership, nationalism and the importance of the state over the individual.

garrison A group of troops placed to defend a location.

Holocaust The systematic German campaign to exterminate millions of Jews and others.

hygiene Following practices, such as keeping clean, that support the maintenance of good health.

independence The state of self-government for a people or nation.

infantry Soldiers who are trained to fight on foot, or in vehicles.

kamikaze Japanese for "divine wind"; the name refers to Japan's suicide pilots.

landing craft Shallow-bottomed boats designed to carry troops and supplies from ships to the shore.

Marine A soldier who serves in close association with naval forces.

materiel A word that describes all the equipment and supplies used by military forces.

morale A sense of common purpose and positive spirits among a group of people or a whole population

occupation The seizure and control of an area by military force.

offensive A planned military attack.

patriotism A love for and promotion of one's country.

propaganda Material such as images, broadcasts or writings that aims to influence the ideas or behaviour of a group of people.

rationing A system of limiting food and other supplies to ensure that everyone gets a similar amount.

reconnaissance A small-scale survey of enemy territory to gather information.

resources Natural materials that are the basis of economic wealth, such as oil, rubber, and agricultural produce.

strategy A detailed plan for achieving success.

strongpoint Any defensive position that has been strengthened to withstand an attack.

siege A military blockade of a place, such as a city, to force it to surrender.

taxes Fees on earnings or financial transactions used by governments to raise money from their citizens.

troops Groups of soldiers.

war bonds A form of investment used by governments in wartime to raise money from savers.

Further Reading

Books

Adams, Simon. *Occupation and Resistance* (Documenting World War II). Wayland, 2008.

Black, Hermann. *World War II, 1939–1945* (Wars Day-by-Day). Brown Bear Reference, 2008.

The Blitz. World War II Replica Memorabilia Pack. Resources for Teaching, 2010.

Burgan, Michael. *America in World War II* (Wars That Changed American History). World Almanac Library, 2006.

Cross, Vince. *Blitz: a Wartime Girl's Diary, 1940–1941* (My Story). Scholastic, 2008.

Deary, Terry, and Mike Phillips. *The Blitz* (Horrible Histories Handbooks). Scholastic 2009.

Dowswell, Paul. *Usborne Introduction to the Second World War.* Usborne Publishing Ltd., 2005.

Gardiner, Juliet. *The Children's War: The Second World War Through the Eyes of the Children of Britain.* Portrait, 2005.

Heppelwhite, Peter. *An Evacuee's Journey* (History Journeys). Wayland, 2004.

Hosch, William L. *World War II: People, Politics and Power* (America at War). Rosen Education Service, 2009.

MacDonald, Fiona. *World War II: Life on the Home Front: A Primary Source History* (In Their Own Words). Gareth Stevens Publishing, 2009.

McNeese, Tim. *World War II: 1939–1945* (Discovering U.S. History). Chelsea House Publishers, 2010.

O'Shei, Tim. *World War II Spies.* Edge Books, 2008.

Price, Sean. *Rosie the Riveter: Women in World War II.* Raintree, 2008.

Price, Sean. *The Art of War: The Posters of World War II* (American History Through Primary Sources). Raintree, 2008.

Ross, Stuart. *The Blitz* (At Home in World War II). Evans Brothers, 2007.

Ross, Stuart. *Evacuation* (At Home in World War II). Evans Brothers, 2007.

Ross, Stuart. *Rationing* (At Home in World War II). Evans Brothers, 2007.

Tonge, Neil. *The Rise of the Nazis* (Documentary World War II). Wayland, 2008.

Wagner, Melissa, and Dan Bryant. *The Big Book of World War II: Fascinating Facts about World War II Including Maps, Historic Photographs and Timelines.* Perseus Books, 2009.

World War II (10 volumes). Grolier Educational, 2006.

World War II (Eyewitness). Dorling Kindersley, 2007.

Websites

www.bbc.co.uk/history/worldwars/wwtwo/
Causes, events and people of the war.

http://www.bbc.co.uk/schools/primaryhistory/world_war2/
Interactive information on what it was like to be a child during the war.

http://www.spartacus.schoolnet.co.uk/2WW.htm
Spartacus Education site on the war.

http://www.nationalarchives.gov.uk/education/worldwar2/
U.S. National Archives primary sources on the war.

http://www.historylearningsite.co.uk/WORLD%20WAR%20TWO.htm
History Learning Site guide to the war.

http://www.telegraph.co.uk/news/newstopics/world-war-2/
Daily Telegraph archive of articles from wartime and from the 70th anniversary of its outbreak.

www.war-experience.org
The Second World War Experience Centre.

www.ibiblio.org/pha
A collection of primary World War II source materials.

www.worldwar-2.net
Complete World War II day-by-day timeline.

http://www.iwm.org.uk/searchlight/server.php?change=SearchlightGalleryView&changeNav=home
Imperial War Museum, London, guide to collections.

Index